A guide to the Care Standards Act 2000

Jon Brand and Peter Fletcher

National Housing Federation and the
National Institute for Social Work

While all reasonable care and attention has been taken in preparing this guide, the National Housing Federation regrets that it cannot assume responsibility for any errors or omissions.

© National Housing Federation

ISBN 0 86297 452 6

First published in December 2000
by the National Housing Federation
175 Gray's Inn Road, London WC1X 8UP

Typesetting Fiona Shand

Printed in Great Britain by Icom Ltd, Unit 28 Bermondsey Trading Estate, Rotherhithe New Road, London SE16 3LL

Contents

Acknowledgements

We would like to thank those people who provided us with comments on the draft of this guide, and whose names are listed below. Their advice was most helpful in helping us finalise the guide.

We would also like to thank our commissioners, Sue Ramsden from the National Housing Federation and Daphne Statham from NISW, whose guidance we have welcomed.

Don Brand and Peter Fletcher
Peter Fletcher Associates
December 2000

List of individuals and organisations that provided comments on the draft guide

Nadra Ahmed	National Care Homes Association
Tony Bennett	Department of Health
Kathleen Boyle	National Housing Federation
Linda Convery	Lewis Silkin Solicitors
Trish Davies	Department of Health
Fahmeeda Gill	National Housing Federation
Chris Greathead	New Leaf
Chris Hume	Department of Health
Des Kelly	BUPA
Bill McCliment	United Kingdom Home Care Association
Barry Newitt	Central & Cecil Housing Trust
Eddie Proctor	Anchor Trust
Bill Puddicombe	Phoenix House
Sue Ramsden	National Housing Federation
Daphne Statham	National Institute for Social Work
Christine Storrs	Look Ahead Housing and Care
Nigel Walker	Housing 21
Liz Woodeson	Department of Health

Foreword

Both the National Housing Federation and the National Institute for Social Work welcome the Care Standards Act 2000 as a milestone in promoting decent service and workforce standards for the care and support of vulnerable people in our society. Although some of the standards will be challenging for providers and require time to prepare for, we believe that the framework and standards set out in the Act, and in subsequent regulations, are right and proper in a civilised society where vulnerable people should have equal rights to the rest of the population.

We therefore believe that service providers in the 'not-for-profit' and 'for-profit' independent sector should welcome the provisions in the Act. It is in this light that we are collaborating together to produce this guide. The aim is to assist providers, and others, such as service commissioners and regulators, to prepare for the implementation of the Act and the regulations that will follow it.

Jim Coulter
Chief Executive
National Housing Federation

Daphne Statham
Director
National Institute for Social Work

Introduction

This guide to the Care Standards Act 2000 is written to explain how the Act will affect all voluntary (including registered social landlords) and private sector providers of care and support services for adults, including residential and nursing homes, domiciliary care and sheltered and supported housing schemes. The term 'independent sector provider' is used to encompass all these types of provider.

The Act is highly significant for service users, commissioners, providers, planners and regulators in the social care, health and housing sectors. It will affect large numbers of registered social landlords and managing agents, as well as private and voluntary organisations and local authorities. It represents a clear departure from the current regulatory framework set by the Registered Homes Act 1984 and the Registered Homes (Amendment) Act 1991. It also reflects the Government's wider objective, seen in initiatives such as Fair Access to Care, to achieve higher and more consistent quality standards throughout the country.

The new regulatory framework set out in the Act has a number of parts, but it needs to be seen as a whole. It brings together in one co-ordinated system the regulation of service standards, regulation of the social care workforce, and regulation of education and training standards in social work and social care. This integrated approach should help to drive up standards of provision and practice, and increase public confidence in care and support services.

The Act brings major changes to the way that care will be regulated, by introducing a new approach for services currently regulated, such as residential and nursing home care; extending regulation to major new areas, particularly domiciliary care (and at a later stage day care); and changing the structures of regulation and standard-setting through establishing new national bodies. The Act also has major new provisions relating to services for children, private health care, and new arrangements in Wales. These are not covered in this guide, which concentrates on social care services for adults and arrangements in England.

The Act received Royal Assent in July 2000, and is being implemented in stages during 2001-2002 and beyond. Much of the detail of how it will operate will be defined in regulations, normally published in draft for consultation, and in associated codes, national minimum standards and occupational standards, which themselves will be the subject of consultation. These can be updated and adapted to the changing context of service provision and public expectations.

This guide should therefore be read by providers as a starting point in preparing for the implementation of the Act. It highlights the areas they need to be thinking about and planning for, and further information to look out for. Chapter 1 outlines the policy aims and main provisions of the Act. Chapter 2 deals with the regulation and registration of services, and Chapter 3 with regulation, registration and training of staff. Chapter 4 examines some of the more complex key issues relating to the Act which are of significance to the independent sector, and outlines conclusions, key actions and preparation points for service providers.

1 Policy context and key provisions

This chapter sets out the policy aims and context of the Care Standards Act 2000, and outlines its key provisions.

The main purpose of the Act is to reform the system for regulating care services in England and Wales. It applies to a range of services from residential and nursing homes and domiciliary care to children's services and private and voluntary health care provision. For the first time, local authorities providing care services will be required to meet the same standards as independent sector providers.

In its White Paper *Modernising Social Services* (1998) the Government set out 'key principles which should underlie high quality, effective services':

- care should be provided to people in a way that supports their independence and respects their dignity;

- services should meet each individual's specific needs, and people should have a say in what services they get and how they are delivered;

- care services should be organised, accessed, provided and financed in a fair, open and consistent way in every part of the country;

- every person should be safeguarded against abuse, neglect or poor treatment whilst receiving care. Where abuse does take place, the system should take firm action to put a stop to it;

- people who receive social services should have an assurance that the staff they deal with are sufficiently trained and skilled for the work they are doing;

- people should be able to have confidence in social care services, knowing they work to clear and acceptable standards.

The Care Standards Act 2000 seeks to implement these principles. It puts in place significant changes to the current system of regulation of care services in England:

- It repeals the Registered Homes Act 1984 and the Registered Homes (Amendment) Act 1991, and replaces local authority and health registration and inspection units with a National Care Standards Commission and a new framework of national service standards. The Commission will register and inspect care homes and domiciliary care agencies, as well as a range of other services.

- It brings domiciliary care services under a national system of registration and regulation for the first time, and other services, including day care, will be incorporated into the framework of the Act at a later stage, via regulations.

- It establishes the General Social Care Council as the new body to regulate the workforce providing social care via registers of staff with approved training, and codes of conduct and practice for staff and employers.

- It sets out a new system to strengthen protection for vulnerable adults.

The Government's objective of developing a new regulatory framework for social care needs to be seen within a broader set of policy objectives and quality measures. Some of these are set out in *Modernising Social Services* and others in related legislation and guidance, examples of which are referred to below. Policy objectives include:

- the reduction in inequalities in society and the promotion of health and well being (The White Paper *Saving Lives: Our Healthier Nation*, 1999);

- the promotion of active citizenship, and the rights and responsibilities of citizens to help themselves (*Better Government for Older People* pilot programme, 1998-2000);

- the promotion of independence and social inclusion for service users, and the shift of emphasis to prevention;

- support for families and carers (*National Strategy for Carers*, 1999);

- a user-centred approach to assessment and service provision;

- improved protection for children, vulnerable adults and the public;

- greater consistency nation-wide in terms of access to and quality of services, and the growing use of charters as one vehicle for this (*Fair Access to Care Services*; *Better Care, Higher Standards*);

- the promotion of partnership working between social services and health (the partnership arrangements in the Health Act 1999) and of the wider partnership agenda – across housing, social services, health, employment and training;

- new administrative and funding arrangements for support services (*Supporting People* 1999);

- modernisation of social care services, set within a wider context of modernising local government (White Paper, *Modernising Local Government, In Touch with the People*, 1998);

- the promotion of knowledge-based practice in the social care field as well as the health sector (*Quality Strategy for Social Care*, 2000);

- the increased focus on outcome measures, sometimes crossing a range of services, rather than narrow performance indicators (the Audit Commission's proposed *Quality of Life and Cross-Cutting Indicators*);

- increased access to education, training and lifelong learning, and establishment of the Learning and Skills Council.

The Care Standards Act 2000, therefore, fits within this wider policy framework and direction. The Supporting People programme will fundamentally change the commissioning, funding and monitoring of supported and sheltered housing. The two new systems do overlap, and much work remains to be done to ensure the outcome is co-ordinated. The Act, which covers aspects of *Modernising Social Services* requiring primary legislation – new regulatory bodies, prescribed national standards, protection requirements – needs to be seen in the context of other related measures. These include:

- the new quality structures in the National Health Service (NHS) – The National Institute for Clinical Excellence and Commission for Health Improvement;

- new functions and approaches undertaken by the Audit Commission and the Housing Corporation;

- the development of the Training Organisation for the Personal Social Services (TOPSS) National Training Strategy for social care and national occupational standards;

- training reforms in the new Quality Strategy for social care;

- the development of national service and performance standards, the Better Regulation Taskforce recommendations, the Performance Assessment Framework (PAF), the Supporting People quality and monitoring framework and Best Value reviews.

2 Regulation and registration of services

This chapter of the guide sets out the main provisions of the Act regarding the regulation and registration of services. Key points for independent sector providers are highlighted using a tick and text in bold.

2.1 Key changes to service regulation

Parts I and II of the Care Standards Act 2000 establish a new framework for the regulation, registration and inspection of care services. The Act will:

- remove from local authorities and health authorities their current responsibilities for registration and inspection, and replace and repeal the Registered Homes Act 1984;

- establish the National Care Standards Commission as the statutory national body for regulating services in England;

- replace the distinction between residential and nursing homes with a single category of care home;

- introduce new definitions of 'personal care' applying to care homes and domiciliary care;

- extend regulation to local authority care homes, and local authority and independent sector domiciliary care agencies;

- enable other services, such as day care, to be brought within the regulatory framework at a later stage;

- enable Ministers to prescribe national minimum standards for different services;

- create a new mechanism for appeals against registration decisions.

Similar changes will apply in Wales, where the registration authority will be a department or agency of the National Assembly. The Act also introduces new arrangements for the registration and inspection of children's services and private health care provision. These changes are not covered in this guide.

2.2 Rationale for changing from the Registered Homes Act 1984 framework

At present, the Registered Homes Act 1984 regulates residential care homes and nursing homes in the private and voluntary sectors (as well as mental nursing homes and private hospitals). It makes the local authority the registration and inspection authority for residential homes, and the health authority for nursing homes. Those dissatisfied with the registration authorities' decisions can appeal to a Registered Homes Tribunal.

Local authorities were required to establish independent inspection and registration units, separate from the line management of services, as part of the *Caring for People* community care reforms of the early 1990s. The units are responsible for inspecting local authority as well as independent sector homes, with advisory groups on which providers and service users are represented. In some areas, the local authority and health authority have established joint inspection units inspecting both residential and nursing homes.

Despite measures to increase the independence of the local units, concerns have persisted. Some have questioned whether the units apply standards even-handedly to local authority and private homes, and quoted instances of perceived bias against private care. Others have suggested conflicts of interest are inevitable when local authorities are at the same time providers, purchasers and regulators of residential care. In addition, regional and national providers (as well as the Government) have been concerned at the seemingly unjustifiable differences in the standards adopted by sometimes neighbouring authorities. Further concerns have included the split of nursing and residential homes into separate systems regulated by the health and local authority respectively, and the seeming focus of the inspection process on building and safety issues rather than on the standards of care.

In 1996, Tom Burgner's influential review of inspection and registration arrangements in England and Wales (Department of Health and Welsh Office, 1996) criticised '*the limited scope of the coverage of regulation; inconsistency in its application; ...weakness in enforcement; and lack of clarity and apparent arbitrariness in determining costs and fee levels*'. He recommended '*a stronger national input into setting standards of care and for registration and inspection methodology and training*'.

The Care Standards Act 2000 addresses these concerns by setting up a new national system of regulation.

2.3 The National Care Standards Commission

Under the Act, the National Care Standards Commission (NCSC) will be the body which registers and inspects social care services in England. As a non-departmental public body, it will have statutory powers and be subject to the directions of Ministers, who will appoint the chair and members of the Commission. They will form the governing body for the Commission, which will be independent of the Department of Health and operate at arm's length from Government. Members of the Commission will be people with a range of experience and interests in social care, including service users and providers. The NCSC will exist in shadow form from April 2001, and will come fully into operation as the national registration body in April 2002. In the first edition of a periodic Newsletter on the NCSC, published on the Department of Health's website, the Minister described the NCSC as *'a powerful new body to raise standards of care and protect vulnerable people. It will be a champion of quality care and a powerful force against poor practice.'* As well as its registration and inspection role, the Commission will have general duties to:

- monitor the availability and quality of care services, including market trends and new developments, and keep Ministers informed;

- encourage improvement in the quality of care services, by giving advice to providers and disseminating examples of good practice;

- provide the public with information on care services, including the types and location of services available and the results of inspections;

- give advice to Ministers on changes needed in national standards, and other matters as required.

Although the Commission will be a national body, the Department of Health intends that it should have a regional structure, probably based on the eight NHS regions. The NCSC will have a Chief Executive, a Children's Rights Director and Regional Directors, as well as a Director of Private and Voluntary Health Care. Inspection and registration staff currently employed in local authority units will be able to transfer to the NCSC. It will work closely with the Commission for Health Improvement, which inspects NHS provision, and the two bodies can exchange staff.

2.4 National, regional and local structures

It is expected that the NCSC will be a three-tiered organisation with national, regional and local offices.

The role of the National Office will include:

- co-ordination with other national bodies such as the General Social Care Council and the Social Services Inspectorate;

- review and development of inspection and regulation methodology to ensure a consistent national approach;

- reporting to Ministers on the quality and range of care services;

- monitoring the NCSC's performance and quality of work.

Regional offices will be small, and will focus on supporting local offices, ensuring consistent inspection and registration practice across the region, and liaison with other regional bodies. They are likely to be responsible for staff appointments, financial, legal and information technology (IT) support to local offices, training and staff development.

Around 80 local offices are envisaged, providing information to the public, access for complaints and for local networking, and a point of contact for inspectors and other NCSC staff who in many cases will be home-based and peripatetic. The majority of the Commission's staff will be working at local level. The local offices will focus on registration, inspection, enforcement, investigation of complaints and servicing local advisory panels

☑ **All independent sector care home and domiciliary care agency providers will need to work closely with their local office of the NCSC, and establish their points of contact with key personnel as the new organisation is set up.**

2.5 Services to be regulated
Care homes

The Care Standards Act 2000 does away with the distinction in the Registered Homes Act 1984 between residential homes and nursing homes...It also makes no reference to the provision of 'board', which was a criterion of registration under the Registered Homes Act 1984.

Under s3 of the new Act, an establishment is a care home if it provides accommodation together with nursing or personal care for any person who:

- is or has been ill;

- has or has had a mental disorder;

- is disabled or infirm;

- is or has been dependent on alcohol or drugs.

The Act requires all care homes to be registered with the NCSC. The Commission will be able to place conditions on care homes, defining the categories of resident they can accommodate. The staffing and skill-mix of each care home will need to be tailored to the assessed needs of its residents.

The term 'personal care' is not defined in the Act, although it does give Ministers power to make regulations excluding particular activities from the meaning of personal care (s121(3)). It will be possible to exclude, through regulation, particular activities that might be considered to amount to personal care. This could vary according to the service provided. Instead of a single definition, the term 'personal care' will take its meaning from the context in the Act, as the paragraph below on care homes illustrates.

In the case of care homes, the meaning of personal care is very wide, and can include a whole range of physical help and emotional care. For an establishment to be a registrable care home, however, the Act makes clear that 'the care which it provides must include assistance with bodily functions' (such as feeding, bathing and toileting) 'where such assistance is required' (s121(9)). The key point is that such assistance must be available, even if it is only rarely required and provided. This essentially replicates the requirement in the 1984 Act. See Chapter 4 for a discussion of the implications of this change.

☑ **All residential and nursing home providers will need to plan for the implications of the new single care home, and consider how best to relate staffing requirements to the needs of their residents.**

Domiciliary care agencies

Under s4(3), a domiciliary care agency is any agency which provides or arranges personal care in their own home to people who are unable to provide it for themselves without assistance because of illness, infirmity or disability. In this case, personal care is limited to physical assistance, although it could cover a wider range of activities than 'assistance with bodily functions' and include, for instance, help to get out of the bath or get dressed. All domiciliary care agencies must register with the NCSC.

Any personal care involving physical assistance delivered to people in supported and sheltered housing will be regulated under this part of the Act. Where domiciliary care is provided to tenants by a care agency, it is the agency, not the landlord, which will be required to register with the NCSC.

☑ **All domiciliary care agencies providing personal care will, for the first time, be subject to national regulation, under the Act.**

☑ **Owners of supported and sheltered/very sheltered housing (not currently regulated through the 1984 Act) who provide personal care, either directly or by arrangement with a care agency, will need to identify how the new requirements for regulating domiciliary care agencies will affect them and their care providers.**

Other regulated services

This guide is mainly concerned with the regulation of care homes and domiciliary care, but these are only part of the NCSC's remit under the Act. It will also regulate children's homes, fostering and adoption agencies and services, independent hospitals and clinics, medical agencies and nurses' agencies, and inspect boarding schools. In due course, registration will also be extended to day centres if they provide personal care.

☑ **It is unlikely that registered social landlords will be affected by these other categories of regulation under the Act, unless they are running day centres or a nurses' agency.**

☑ **Other independent sector providers of services for adults will be affected if they run any of this wider set of health-related services outlined above.**

2.6 Registration requirements

Part II of the Act deals with the registration of establishments, such as care homes and children's homes, and agencies including those providing domiciliary care.

Applying to register

Section 11 makes it an offence for anyone to carry on or manage an establishment or agency without being registered with the NCSC. There must be a registered person carrying on each care home or agency. If that person is not in day-to-day charge, under the Act the manager must also be registered. An agency operating from several branches must register each branch separately (s11(2)).

The framework for applying to be registered is set out in s12. A person applying to be a registered manager must be an individual, not a company or local authority. A company or local authority may however apply to register as the person carrying on the establishment or agency. Applications must be made to the NCSC, and must give information prescribed in regulations and any other information reasonably required by the Commission. A proprietor or manager of more than one home or agency must make a separate application for each one. Regulations under s22 will define the requirements of 'fit persons' to carry on or manage homes or agencies.

Where two separate organisations are involved in the ownership and management of a care home, it will be important to clarify who is 'carrying on' the home.

☑ **Owners of schemes where they are not in day-to-day charge but have a manager, will need to ensure that their manager is able to meet the registration requirements.**

☑ **Where a registered social landlord has a contract with a managing agent, the contract should stipulate who is responsible for the registration requirements.**

Granting, refusing and cancelling registration

Section 13 explains the process for granting or refusing registration. The NCSC will grant registration only if it is satisfied that the person applying has complied, or will comply, with all the requirements of regulations, standards and other relevant legislation. (The areas covered by regulation are set out in s22.) If it is satisfied, it must issue a certificate of registration. If it is not satisfied, the Commission will refuse registration. Under s13(3) the NCSC can attach conditions to the registration, and can vary, remove or add conditions at any time.

Under s14, the NCSC can cancel a registration at any time:

● if a condition of registration or a regulatory requirement has been breached; or

● if a relevant offence has been committed. Relevant offences (see ss24-30 below) include:

    – failure to comply with conditions

    – contravention of regulations

    – false description of an establishment or agency

    – false statements in applications

- failure to display a certificate of registration
- obstructing an inspector.

Cancellation would not normally be the first step in enforcing standards or requirements. It is more likely to be used after other measures, such as prosecution, have been tried and failed. The Commission could pursue both courses of action at the same time, if necessary. The NCSC can cancel an individual's registration even if an owner closes the service before the process of cancellation is complete.

☑ **These sections raise issues of Quality Assurance for owners and managers. They need to have systems in place to ensure that their home or agency complies with the conditions of registration.**

Conditions and regulations

Under s15, the registered person can apply to the NCSC to change the conditions attached to their registration. They may, for example, want approval to alter the number of people the home accommodates. Regulations will set out the information required for the application, and there will be a prescribed fee. If the NCSC grants the application, it will give written notice and issue a new registration certificate.

This section also covers voluntary applications to have a registration cancelled, if, for instance, the registered person is planning to sell or close the home or agency. Section 15(2) prevents the registered person from voluntarily cancelling his or her registration if the NCSC has already decided, or given notice of intention, to cancel the registration.

Section 16 gives Ministers the power to make regulations about registration. Much of the detail about the new system will be contained in regulations, which are issued for consultation before being finalised. Regulations will cover such things as:

- the information which must be provided when applying to register;
- the information which will be contained in registration certificates;
- the level and structure of annual fees for registration, which may be set at different levels for different types of organisation.

☑ **Care providers and their national associations will need to be alert to new sets of draft regulations as they are issued, and to take the opportunity to comment on them if they wish to do so.**

2.7 Registration procedures

The Commission is required to give notice of decisions it intends to take about an application for registration, a cancellation or a change in conditions (s17). This 'notice of proposal' must be given to the applicant or registered person, and must set out the NCSC's reasons for the decision it intends to take, for example, about conditions to be attached to the registration. Notice is not required if the Commission decides to grant an application without conditions, or with conditions agreed with the applicant.

Section 18 gives the person receiving a notice of proposal 28 days to make written representations back to the Commission. This is to make sure the applicant has the opportunity to put forward any views on the decision before it is finalised. The NCSC must not make its decision until it has received the applicant's representations, or written notice that he or she does not intend to make any, or the 28 days have elapsed.

Section 19 covers written notice of decisions by the Commission. Once the representations stage is complete:

- the NCSC will give the person applying written notice of its decision;

- the notice will set out any conditions the NCSC has decided to attach to the registration, or any variation in conditions, and will explain how to appeal;

- if the decision is to cancel the person's registration, or attach or vary conditions which have not been agreed, it will not take effect until any appeal has been determined, or after 28 days if the applicant has not appealed;

- if, during the 28-day period, the applicant notifies the NCSC that he or she does not intend to appeal against the conditions, the decision to grant conditional registration takes effect immediately.

The procedure for urgent cancellation of registration is set out in s20. It enables the Commission to apply to a magistrate for immediate cancellation of a registration, or change in conditions attached to a registration. Before making an order, the magistrate must be satisfied that there is a serious risk to a person's life, health or well-being unless the order is made. There will be a fast-track procedure for appeals to the Tribunal against such an order.

Under s20(3), the NCSC must notify the local authority, health authority and any other relevant authority that it is making an urgent application. This is to allow the authorities to make any alternative arrangements which may be necessary.

Section 21 allows an appeal against an NCSC decision to the Tribunal established under s9 of the Protection of Children Act 1999. Appeals must be brought within 28 days of receiving notice of a decision or order. On hearing the appeal, the Tribunal can:

- confirm the NCSC decision or magistrate's order;

- direct that the decision or order does not have effect;

- vary or cancel an existing condition;

- attach any condition it thinks fit.

☑ **Providers should be familiar with the Commission's procedures and timescales for giving notice, receiving representations and notifying decisions, and with appeals arrangements.**

2.8 Regulations and standards

The Act gives Ministers powers under s22 to make regulations about homes and agencies. Regulations can cover:

- management requirements, including operational management and control arrangements, the definition of 'fit persons' to carry on or manage homes and agencies, and any requirements about registration of managers with the General Social Care Council;

- staffing requirements, including numbers, types, management and training of staff;

- suitability of premises and provision of facilities and services;

- the welfare of people receiving services, including health protection and promotion, and control and restraint in the management of behaviour;

- the conduct of homes and agencies, including the keeping of records and accounts, notification of events, arrangements for cover during the manager's absence, notifying change of manager or ownership and any associated fees, arrangements for dealing with complaints, and quality standards of any nursing provided.

Consultation will take place on draft regulations or amendments before they take effect.

Section 23 enables Ministers to publish national minimum standards for care homes and domiciliary care agencies, as well as other establishments and agencies. They must keep the standards under review, amending and updating them after consultation as appropriate.

The introduction of national minimum standards is a major change from previous arrangements. The standards will form the basis for inspection of services by NCSC inspectors, and are the means by which the Commission will seek to secure consistent national standards of service provision and management. The Commission must take account of the standards in its decisions on registration matters. They must also be taken into account in proceedings for making an order under emergency procedures, appeals against decisions or orders, and offence proceedings.

Draft standards for care homes for older people were published for consultation under the title *Fit for the Future? National Required Standards for Residential and Nursing Homes for Older People* (Department of Health, 1999). They covered:

- the home's brochure and prospectus;

- rights of individual residents;

- complaints;

- policies, procedures, records and protocols;

- health and personal care;

- daily life and social activities;

- food and meal times;

- dying and death;

- the physical environment;

- management and administration;

- staffing and training requirements.

Following the period of consultation, and extensive debate during the passage of the Care Standards Bill, Ministers are to publish revised standards. On one particularly controversial issue, room sizes, Ministers announced their intentions in advance of the full standards being available. The key facts are set out in the box below to highlight their importance for independent sector providers.

Room size minimum standards in care homes for older people

- There will be a minimum standard of $10m^2$ for single rooms ($12m^2$ for new provision).

- There will be some flexibility in the application of the space standard and the timescale:

  - individual providers will have five years from April 2002, when the NCSC comes into operation, to meet the space standards in existing homes. During the transitional period 2002 to 2007, the space standards will not be enforced on sale or transfer of existing homes to new owners;

  - single room sizes smaller than $10m^2$ will be acceptable if there is compensatory space elsewhere, whether in the form of en suite facilities or additional day space which residents may individually use if they wish. Rooms should not be less than $9.3m^2$, and the total space available to a resident should be not less than $14.1m^2$. Conversely, in homes which do not meet the minimum day-space standard of $4.1m^2$ per resident, but where larger individual rooms compensate, a new lower minimum day-space of $3.7m^2$ will be allowed.

The Department will publish for consultation further draft minimum standards applying to care homes for adults with disabilities, domiciliary care agencies, and other services subject to NCSC regulation.

☑ **The introduction of national minimum standards is a major change from previous arrangements and independent sector providers will need to be alert for new draft regulations, as they are issued, which relate to care home and domiciliary care agency standards.**

☑ *Pr*oviders of residential care and nursing homes should begin to plan now on the issue of **room sizes and shared rooms in care homes to ensure that their homes will meet the required standards set out above by 2007.**

2.9 Offences and enforcement procedures

Sections 24-30 define a number of situations which constitute offences under Part II of the Act, the penalties they carry and the way proceedings are to be brought. The provisions are similar to those in the Registered Homes Act 1984.

Failure to comply with conditions

Under s24 it is an offence if a registered owner or manager fails, without reasonable excuse, to comply with a condition of registration. The penalty is a fine up to level 5 on the standard scale (currently £5,000).

Contravention of regulations

Section 25 allows the regulations made under the Act to provide that it is an offence to contravene or fail to comply with any specified part of the regulations. It is intended that the NCSC will serve notice of a breach of regulations and a requirement to remedy it within a specified period. If it is not remedied, the registered person is guilty of an offence and the penalty is a fine up to level 4 (currently £2,500).

False descriptions

It is an offence under s26 to describe any premises as a particular kind of establishment or agency if it is not registered as such, and if the intention is to deceive other people. This includes, for instance, claiming an unregistered home is registered, or misrepresenting the nature of a registered home by claiming it caters for a particular category of residents, or provides a particular service, when it does not. The penalty is a fine up to level 5.

False statements in applications

Under s27, it is an offence knowingly to make a false or misleading statement in applications to the NCSC to register a home or agency, or vary a condition of registration. The penalty is a fine up to level 4. Application forms will draw attention to this offence, in order to encourage applicants to provide accurate information.

Failure to display registration certificate

Section 28 makes it an offence if the registration certificate is not displayed in a conspicuous place in the home or agency, and the penalty is a fine up to level 2 (currently £500).

Proceedings for offences

Proceedings for offences under Part II of the Act will be brought by the NCSC (s29). The time limit for the NCSC to bring a prosecution is six months from the date on which evidence of the offence comes to its notice. Where such evidence comes to light during an inspection, or through whistle-blowing, some time may have elapsed since the event itself. Prosecution cannot take place more than three years after the offence was committed.

Section 30 applies where an offence has been committed by a body corporate such as a company, a registered charity or a local authority. If an individual officer, such as a director, manager or secretary of the body, has consented to, connived in or contributed through neglect to, the offence, they may be liable to prosecution as well as the company or organisation. In the case of a local authority, this provision may apply to any officer or member.

☑ **Members of authorities, boards and other governing bodies should consider what monitoring and reporting arrangements are necessary to enable them and their managers and staff to discharge their responsibilities effectively.**

2.10 Inspection arrangements

Sections 31 and 32 set out the provisions under which the NCSC will carry out its inspection functions, and the powers of inspectors authorised to act on the Commission's behalf.

Under s31, registered owners and managers of homes are required to provide the Commission with any information it considers necessary to the discharge of its functions. It gives an authorised inspector powers to enter and inspect a home or agency at any time, and to:

- inspect the premises and the care and treatment of people accommodated there;

- require the home or agency to produce for inspection any documents or records prescribed under regulations, wherever they are kept, and allow them to be copied. Where records are kept on computer, they must be made available to inspectors in a form in which they can be read and copied for removal;

- interview in private the manager, proprietor or any member of staff;

- interview, in private and subject to their consent, anyone accommodated and receiving care. If the authorised person carrying out the inspection is a medical practitioner or registered nurse, and believes the resident is not receiving proper care, they have the power, with the individual's consent, to examine them and their medical records. They may do so without consent if the individual is incapable of giving consent.

Other parts of this section:

- provide for regulations to specify the minimum frequency of inspections;

- require inspectors to produce appropriate documentation confirming their rights of entry and inspection;

- make it an offence punishable by a fine to obstruct an authorised inspector or fail to comply with any requirement under this section (eg, the requirement to allow access to the home, or make records available for inspection).

Under s32, an inspector can:

- remove any material or records which may be evidence of failure to comply with requirements;

- require anyone to provide any assistance necessary to enable him or her to carry out duties under Part II of the Act;

- take any measurements, photographs and recordings he or she needs to carry out his or her responsibilities.

After each inspection, the NCSC is required to:

- prepare a report;

- send a copy of the report to each person registered in connection with the home or agency;

- make the report available to the public at the regional office, publicise it as appropriate, and provide copies on request, charging a fee for the copy if it sees fit.

2.11 Administrative requirements
Annual returns

Under s33, regulations may require homes or agencies to make annual returns to the NCSC, and stipulate the information to be supplied, the period to be covered and the date the return is due.

Appointment of liquidators

Regulations under s34 will cover the requirements when a company providing registered services is placed in the hands of a receiver or liquidator, including requirements to notify the NCSC of the appointment and to appoint a suitably qualified manager.

Death of registered person

The requirements in the event of the death of the sole person registered in connection with a home or agency are dealt with in s35.

Provision of copies of registers

Section 36 covers the responsibilities of the NCSC to:

- make copies of registers available for inspection by the public;

- supply a copy of, or extract from, a register on request, either free or for a suitable fee;

- withhold access to the register or copies of it, in circumstances prescribed in regulations.

Service of documents

Section 37 allows a notice or other document to be served either in person, or by registered post or recorded delivery, when it will be taken as served three days after it was sent.

Extending registration to other services

Powers to extend registration to services, such as day care, not included on the face of the Act are provided in s42.

☑ **Providers will need to become familiar with the workings and rights of the NCSC in relation to areas such as inspection, and to their responsibilities and duties to comply with the provisions of the Act and its regulations, for example in the provision of an annual return to the NCSC.**

3 Regulation and training of staff

This chapter of the guide sets out the main provisions of the Act regarding the regulation and training of staff. Key points for independent sector providers are highlighted using a tick and text in bold.

3.1 Current position and key changes

Over a million people work in social care services in England. Many of the children and adults receiving their care and support are vulnerable and at risk. Many service users rely on social workers and social care staff to provide their day-to-day personal care, look after their interests, protect them from harm, or prevent them becoming a danger to themselves or other people.

Up to now there has been no organisation, such as exists in most other professional and caring fields, with the task of regulating standards of conduct and practice for the social care workforce. There has been growing public concern about examples of gross misconduct, bad practice and abuse by a small minority of staff. Serious incidents have occurred in the local authority, private and voluntary sectors, and in services for children, older people, those with physical and sensory disabilities, people with mental health problems and learning disabilities. Inquiries into these events have received widespread publicity, and severely damaged public confidence in social care services and the staff who work in them.

In responding to these concerns, the Care Standards Act 2000:

- sets up the General Social Care Council (GSCC) and the Care Council for Wales (CCW) as the bodies responsible for setting and regulating standards for staff. Similar bodies are to be established in Scotland and Northern Ireland;

- requires the councils to maintain registers of social care staff, develop codes of practice for staff and employers, and regulate social work training;

- enables the title of 'social worker' to be protected;

- abolishes the Central Council for Education and Training in Social Work (CCETSW), the current regulator of social work training, and transfers its functions to the GSCC, the CCW and their Scottish and Northern Ireland counterparts;

- gives Ministers responsibility for ascertaining the training needs of the social care workforce, drawing up occupational standards, and promoting social care training; and allows the powers to be delegated to the Training Organisation for the Personal Social Services (TOPSS) England;

- introduces a new system for listing staff who are considered unsuitable to work with vulnerable adults, with requirements on employers to check and notify. A similar system to prevent unsuitable people working with children was enacted in the Protection of Children Act 1999.

3.2 General Social Care Council

Under s54 of the Act, the General Social Care Council is to be the statutory body for regulating and registering social care staff in England. Like the NCSC, it will be a non-departmental body with statutory powers, independent of the Department of Health but operating under the direction and guidance of the Secretary of State, who will appoint the chair and members of the Council. Its size is unlikely to exceed 25 people. The Council is due to come formally into operation in October 2001.

The Government has stated that the Council will have a lay chair and a majority of lay members, including at least two service users as well as carers and people representing the public interest. Service user interests will be consulted before appointments are made to the Council, and applications will be invited from the public. Other members will reflect the range of interests in social care, including employers, staff, professional and trades union bodies, and education and training providers.

The Act defines the task of the GSCC as promoting:

- high standards of conduct and practice among social care workers;

- high standards in their training.

It gives the Council general powers to carry out its functions, and a specific power to co-operate with other public authorities. This includes the councils which will be the GSCC's counterparts in Scotland, Wales and Northern Ireland. Ministers expect the four councils to work closely with one another in ways which help to protect the public, such as the exchange of information about people refused registration or removed from a council's register. They also have scope to co-operate with regulatory bodies in allied fields, such as teaching, nursing, counselling and the health professions.

3.3 Codes of conduct and practice

Section 62 requires the councils to prepare and publish codes of good practice for social care staff and employers. Drawing up and consulting widely on these codes will be the first task for the GSCC and the other councils. Work has begun to prepare draft codes for consideration and further development by the councils as they come into existence.

Once the codes are agreed, they will be published and promoted by the councils. They will give guidance to staff, employers, service users and the public about the standards of conduct and practice expected of people working in social care, and the responsibilities of employers to ensure those standards are maintained.

Conduct and practice requirements are likely to change and develop over time, as the knowledge-base for social care expands, social care practice develops and public and user expectations rise. The Council will have a duty to keep the codes under review, and amend the standards as necessary, in consultation with staff and other interests as appropriate.

Code of practice for staff

The code of practice for staff must be adhered to by all social care workers, not just those required to register with the GSCC at an early stage. It is likely to be incorporated into terms and conditions of employment for all social care workers, including those working in care homes or employed by a domiciliary care agency to provide personal care. The code will set out the principles of good conduct expected from social care workers in their work with service users. Its purpose is to set and maintain high standards of conduct and practice, to protect the rights and well-being of those who use the services of social care staff, and to ensure that staff do not exploit or abuse the position of trust in which they are placed.

The code will also provide the basis for decisions by the GSCC on matters of misconduct, and must be taken into account in appeal proceedings against GSCC decisions. Ministers can direct local authorities to take the code into account in decisions about the conduct of social care workers they employ.

Code of practice for employers

The code of practice for employers will set out their responsibilities for ensuring staff are able to work in ways which are consistent with the GSCC's standards. It will include good practice in the recruitment, selection and appointment of staff, their induction and ongoing training, and the provision of management support and supervision. It will also cover the duties of employers to ensure staff do not abuse their position, and the action to be taken if serious misconduct or abuse is discovered or suspected.

The Government has stated that the codes will be included in the minimum standards for regulated services, and inspections by the National Care Standards Commission will examine the arrangements made by service providers to implement the codes. For staff registered with the GSCC, adherence to the Council's standards of conduct and competence will be a condition of admission to the register and a requirement for their continuing registration. Appropriate links will be made between the GSCC's standards and the national occupational standards approved by TOPSS.

☑ **All employers of social care staff will have to adopt the new codes of conduct and practice, which will be a part of the Government's minimum standards for regulated services.**

☑ **Providers should ensure their views are reflected in responses to consultation on the draft codes.**

☑ **Providers will need to ensure they are able to comply with the requirements in the employers' code, and have robust systems in place to support good practice and deal with breaches of the code of practice by their staff.**

3.4 Register of social care workers

Section 56 requires the GSCC to maintain a register of social workers and other groups of social care workers. The register will be the principal mechanism by which the GSCC regulates standards of conduct and practice among social care staff. Those registered with the Council will be accountable for adhering to its codes and standards, and in the event of serious misconduct may be subject to the GSCC's disciplinary procedures, which can lead to suspension or removal from the register.

The Act provides that there will be a part of the register for social workers and other parts for other categories of social care staff as specified by Ministers. They are likely to adopt an incremental approach, extending registration to additional categories of staff over a period of time. Social workers will be the first group registered, probably in 2002. Registered managers of care homes and residential child care staff are also likely to become eligible for registration at an early stage. Ministers also have the power to order the closure of a part of the register.

Social care workers, as defined in s55, include:

- social workers (ie, those engaged in 'relevant social work' in connection with any health, education or social services function);

- staff who work in children's homes, care homes or residential family centres;

- staff who work for or are supplied by domiciliary care agencies to provide personal care;

- managers of such homes, centres and agencies.

Regulations may lead to other categories of staff being treated as social care workers for purposes of registration, including:

- individuals providing personal care for any person;

- NCSC inspectors and their managers;

- day centre workers;

- social work students.

Section 69 requires the GSCC to publish its register, and make a copy or extract available to anyone who asks for one.

☑ **All social care staff employed in care homes and domiciliary care agencies will eventually come under these new regulations. Registration will be phased in as levels of training** increase, and will in due course cover the whole social care workforce. Registered managers of care homes will be among the early groups for whom registration is provided.

3.5 Registration procedures

Section 57 deals with applications for registration, and s58 with granting or refusing admission to the register. The GSCC will make rules about how social care workers should apply for admission, and the requirements they must meet. All the Council's rules have to be approved by Ministers.

Department of Health Ministers have indicated that they intend completion of approved training to be a condition of admission to the GSCC's register. Registration is likely to be open first to social workers, most of whom hold a recognised professional qualification. Residential child care staff and managers of care homes are other groups likely to receive priority for inclusion in registration procedures.

Applicants will have to specify in which part or parts of the register they wish to be registered, The GSCC will grant the application if it is satisfied that the applicant:

- is of good character;

- is physically and mentally fit to perform all or part of the work to which that part of the register relates;

- meets relevant training requirements laid down by the Council;

- meets any competence and conduct requirements set by the Council.

If the GSCC is not satisfied on any count it will refuse the application. The application can be granted unconditionally or with conditions attached.

The GSCC has power to make rules about registration of staff under s60. Rules can cover:

- the keeping of the register;

- documentary and other evidence to accompany applications for registration or variations in the register entry;

- the length of the period of registration, and requirements for renewing registration.

Section 71 gives the GSCC further powers, subject to the consent of Ministers, to make rules about payment of fees, including fees for registration and periodic fees for remaining on the register.

☑ **Care providers will need to get to know the rules about registration, and to set up systems to ensure that staff working in care homes and domiciliary care agencies are able to register with the GSCC when relevant sections of the register are opened and registration becomes a requirement.**

3.6 Removal from the register

Arrangements for an individual's suspension or removal from the GSCC's register are set out in s59. This action is likely to arise as a result of investigations into serious misconduct or other breaches of the Council's requirements by the person registered.

The Council's rules, approved by Ministers, will set out the circumstances and procedures under which:

- an individual can be removed from a part of the register, temporarily or permanently, or restored to that part of the register after a period of removal;

- an individual's registration can be suspended for a specified period, or the suspension terminated;

- an entry in a part of the register can be removed, altered or restored.

The Council will also prescribe the procedure and rules of evidence for proceedings to consider an individual's suspension, removal or restoration. The proceedings will be in public unless the rules specify otherwise.

3.7 Protection of vulnerable adults

Part VII of the Act introduces new measures to protect vulnerable adults. It requires the Secretary of State for Health to maintain a list of people considered unsuitable to work with vulnerable adults, whether in a paid or unpaid capacity. Their names will be placed on the list if they are found to have caused harm or risk of harm to a vulnerable adult. 'Harm' is defined under s121(1) as 'ill-treatment or impairment of health', and in the case of an adult who is mentally impaired, includes impairment of their development.

The provisions for the protection of vulnerable adults (PoVA) are likely to be implemented from April 2002. When this part of the Act comes into force, employers of care workers will be required to check that a prospective employee is not on the list, and if they are, to refuse them employment. Access to checks will be available in due course via the Criminal Records Bureau. Existing care workers found to be on the list will not be able to continue working in care positions. It will be an offence for a person on the list to seek or accept work in a care position.

Definition of 'care worker'

Section 80 defines a care worker, for the purposes of Part VII of the Act, as a person who is employed in a position:

- giving regular contact with residents of a care home or people receiving prescribed services in the NHS or private health services; or

- concerned with providing personal care to people in their own homes.

The definition of 'care worker' in this section is broader than the definition of 'social care worker' in s55. The definition includes supply workers provided by an agency, and temporary staff. It includes volunteers as well as paid staff.

'Vulnerable adults' as defined in s80(6) include any resident in a care home, and anyone receiving personal care in their own home from a domiciliary care agency.

List of people unsuitable to work with vulnerable adults

Section 81 places a duty on the Secretary of State to keep a list of individuals considered unsuitable to work with vulnerable adults. A person can only be included if referred under the provisions of Part VII, and the Secretary of State can remove a person from the list if satisfied he or she should not have been included.

Duty of providers of care services to refer care workers to the list

Providers of care services are required under s82 to refer a care worker to the list if:

- they have dismissed the worker on grounds of misconduct which caused a vulnerable adult harm or risk of harm;

- the worker has resigned, retired or been made redundant before the employer dismissed him or her on those grounds;

- they have, on those grounds, transferred the worker to other work;

- they have suspended or provisionally transferred them to other work.

If information about a care worker causing harm or risk of harm comes to light after they have resigned, been dismissed or transferred, the employer is still required to refer the person to the list.

Referrals are required only in cases where the dismissal or resignation took place after commencement of this section of the Act.

On referral, if the Secretary of State considers listing may be appropriate, the individual is provisionally placed on the list while the referral is under consideration. The person referred and the provider will each be invited to make observations about the information provided by the other, and to comment on each other's observations. The person referred will not be able to work as a care worker whilst provisionally listed.

The Secretary of State will take all the available information into account in deciding whether he or she is satisfied:

- it was reasonable for the provider to consider the worker guilty of misconduct;

- the person is unsuitable to work with vulnerable adults.

If he or she is satisfied, the person's name will be confirmed on the list. If not, it will be removed.

Section 83 sets out similar requirements for employment agencies to refer supply workers under the appropriate circumstances.

The NCSC can refer a worker to the list if it comes across evidence of misconduct in an inspection which has not been referred to the list by the employer (s84). This may arise where a home has closed and the owner is refusing to co-operate, or where the owner has caused harm to vulnerable adults.

Section 85 deals with individuals named in the findings of certain types of inquiry who are found guilty of relevant misconduct, and to whom similar considerations apply.

Appeals against inclusion in the list

Individuals have a right of appeal against being included in the list, but not against provisional inclusion whilst the relevant inquiries are being made (s86).

Appeal is to the Tribunal established under the Protection of Children Act 1999. The Tribunal must be satisfied both that the individual was guilty of misconduct, and that he or she is unsuitable to work with vulnerable adults. If not satisfied on either ground, the Tribunal will allow the appeal, and the individual's name will be removed from the list. Where the person has been convicted of an offence involving misconduct, the Tribunal cannot challenge the facts on which the conviction was based.

Section 87 allows individuals to apply to the Tribunal for their name to be removed from the list under certain conditions. Under s88, applications for removal can be made only:

- with the leave of the Tribunal;

- after the individual has been permanently listed for 10 years, or five years if he or she was aged under 18 when listed;

- if unsuccessful, at 10-yearly intervals after that, or five-yearly if he or she was under 18.

The Tribunal will decide whether or not he or she remains unsuitable to work with vulnerable adults.

Effects on employers and the individual of inclusion in the list

Under s89, providers of registered care homes and domiciliary services must check that a prospective employee is not on the list before offering them employment in a care capacity. If they find the person is listed, they must not employ them. Where workers are supplied by an employment agency, the provider can obtain written confirmation that the agency has carried out the checks in the last 12 months. If the employer discovers a worker is listed, employment must cease.

Under s89(5), it will be an offence liable to imprisonment for anyone confirmed on the list to apply for, accept or work in a care position.

Under s90, the Criminal Records Bureau will be able to include, in a criminal record certificate or enhanced certificate, whether the individual is listed and any details required in regulations. Pending the Bureau taking on its functions, applications for checks will be made to the Secretary of State.

Power to extend Part VII

The provisions for protecting vulnerable adults can be extended by regulations under s93 to take account of changing patterns of service. The definitions of a care provider, a care worker, care position and a vulnerable adult can be amended, and other services such as day care can be brought within these arrangements.

☑ **The new provisions for protection of vulnerable adults will place substantial responsibilities on care providers and employers to ensure unsuitable people are excluded from the workforce and prevent harm to people receiving care.**

☑ **Providers will need to incorporate the new provisions into their personnel policies and recruitment and vetting procedures. They will require robust systems for dealing with allegations of abuse and harm by staff and volunteers, and for managing and notifying dismissals involving harm to vulnerable adults.**

☑ **Providers will need to be aware that these requirements will come into force at a future date, and be alert for further information. They will need to help staff, volunteers and service users understand how the new system will work when a care worker is accused of causing harm.**

3.8 Education and training

Less than 20 per cent of the social care workforce hold a relevant recognised qualification. Large numbers of care staff working in residential and domiciliary care are without relevant qualifications, although the qualification levels are improving. Ministers have expressed their concerns about this position, and their support for concerted action by employers to improve the training of staff in social care. Their 'Quality Strategy for Social Care' states that:

> 'Social care staff comprise the single greatest asset services possess; to make the most of this asset, staff training and development must be overhauled....Modern social care requires a workforce which is better trained, is able to work across service boundaries and

in partnership with service users, continually updates its knowledge and skills, and clearly links training and development to career progression'.

Section 67 of the Act gives Ministers a number of functions in relation to training, and the power to delegate those functions to other bodies. The functions include assessing the training needs of the social care workforce, and the financial support needed to promote such training; encouraging the provision of such support; drawing up occupational standards for social care workers; and promoting social care training by providing information and encouraging recruitment to training programmes.

The body responsible for training strategies and occupational standards for staff and managers in care homes and domiciliary care is the Training Organisation for Personal Social Services. Ministers intend to delegate their functions under s67(5)(b) and to TOPSS England. In autumn 1999, TOPSS England published for consultation its draft National Training Strategy for Social Care *Modernising the Social Care Workforce*. Following consultation, the strategy was finalised in summer 2000, and has been endorsed by Ministers. It is available on the TOPSS England website.

The training strategy sets out key principles and strategic objectives for the period 2000-2005. These include:

- the development of a comprehensive framework of National Occupational Standards for all job roles in social care, and promotion of their use in workforce planning, job definition, training development and performance appraisal;

- a structured induction and foundation programme for all new entrants to the social care workforce;

- training plans for all establishments and agencies, and individual training profiles for all staff;

- all employers to allocate a percentage of their staffing budget to training, and all employees to contribute to their own training;

- national targets and action plans for increasing the levels of qualified staff in all sectors.

National Occupational Standards are being developed or revised for a number of categories of staff, including registered managers of care homes.

The training strategy includes targets for increasing the proportion of care staff in care homes qualified at least to NVQ Level 2 to 50 per cent by 2005. A similar target was included in the draft standards in *Fit for the Future*. Standards for homes for adults and for domiciliary care agencies are likely to include similar requirements for staff training and qualification levels. Set out in the box below is an example of where a partnership or consortia approach to training is already being developed with the aim of increasing the proportion of the care workforce that has some qualifications. The partnership operates across two local authorities as well as the voluntary and private sectors and shows what can be done now.

A training consortium in Hull and East Riding

In Hull and East Riding the two local authorities and independent care agencies have come together with Humberside Training and Enterprise Council (TEC) in a training consortium. They have secured European Union money to help fund a full-time training post. The consortium board is chaired by the TEC and has two local authority representatives, together with two from 'not-for-profit' and two from 'for-profit' independent sector providers. They have registered over 125 participants on NVQ 2 in the past year. Both Hull and East Riding Councils have further subsidised the original grant, which means that independent sector providers can send their staff on training for only 50 per cent of the true cost, as an incentive for them to do so.

☑ Employers in social care are under continuing pressure to improve staff training and development, and to ensure their staff are properly equipped for the responsibilities they carry.

☑ All employers will be encouraged to implement the guidance from TOPSS on induction, training plans and profiles, and to make appropriate provision for the cost of training their staff.

☑ Independent sector providers need to keep under review the current and future training needs of their staff, including the NCSC's requirements for levels of qualified staff as part of their implementation of national standards.

☑ They should also be alert to changes in the pattern of resource provision for training, including funding allocated by the new Learning and Skills Council.

4 Some implications of the Act

In Chapters 2 and 3 we highlighted areas of the new Act which will have implications for independent sector providers. In this final chapter we:

- firstly, examine in more detail four of the more complex key areas of change where providers will need to tease out what the changes will mean for them;

- secondly, outline key conclusions in order to help providers be clear what they can be doing now to prepare for the Act.

4.1 Implications

What are the implications of moving from the distinction between residential homes and nursing homes to a single category of 'care home'?

Many service providers have been frustrated by the current inflexibility and demarcation lines between residential care and nursing homes, even allowing for the ability for a home to be dually registered. Residents in both types of home may require nursing tasks or care, and the level of each may vary according to the health and well-being of individual residents. This has led to uncertainty about whether or not service users should transfer from one category of home to another, as their health and social care needs change over time. Providers have also expressed concerns about providing proper levels of care for residents whose level of need may have changed, but where the contract price from the purchaser has not.

The new single care home definition aims to overcome some of these demarcation lines, and to bring more flexibility and sensitivity into the system for service users, providers and purchasers alike.

However, it will raise a new set of issues for purchasers and providers to address. Instead of classifying a home under a specific category, which is inflexible for purchaser and provider alike, and agreeing a spot or block contract fee for residents based on that classification, local and health authorities could potentially adopt a new, more flexible, contracting system. This would allow for the reassessment of the dependency levels and needs of residents in a scheme on a regular basis. From this purchasers and providers would, in theory, be able to agree an overall dependency profile for the scheme, and for each resident in the scheme. From this information a spot purchase price for each individual or a block purchase price for a scheme as a whole can be assessed.

The aim would be for the overall contract fee income for a scheme to be able to flex and change up or down, on a regular, say quarterly or six monthly basis, to take account of the changing dependency profile in the scheme over a particular period in time.

This could potentially give providers the flexibility of matching income levels from contracts to the changing dependency levels of their residents that is lacking under the current system. However, such a system may be more complicated for both purchasers and providers to manage, need more casual staff, and require a high level of trust that purchasers would be in a position to increase as well as decrease the contract price as care needs changed.

☑ **Government may issue guidance on a common approach to assessing needs and dependency levels for residents, and providers should take part in any opportunity for consultation.**

☑ **It is in the interests of providers to work proactively with health and social services commissioners and other providers to identify ways of addressing dependency level assessment for care homes which they can work with, and which can be used to adjust care plans, define staffing levels and inform the setting of contract prices.**

There is a further set of implications for registered social landlords. The Housing Corporation's funding and monitoring systems are quite different for care homes and nursing homes. Residential care homes fall within the definition of 'social housing' whilst nursing homes are excluded.

Where does supported and sheltered/very sheltered housing fit in the new registration system?

For some providers the definitions of residential care in the 1984 and 1991 Acts seemed outdated and in conflict with concepts of independent living, flexible care (often of a peripatetic nature) based around individual need, and a philosophy of rehabilitation and recuperation rather than one of maintenance. For example, schemes in small shared houses, or schemes focused on intensive support and self-help to promote independence, rather than the provision of personal care, did not seem to fit into the standard mould of residential care, with communal dining rooms, shared bathrooms and 24-hour staffing on site.

Some providers found it difficult to persuade registration and inspection units to adopt a more flexible approach, and not register a scheme where, for example, residents were doing things for themselves, such as providing or cooking meals. This was sometimes the case even where residents were living in fully self-contained accommodation, such as very sheltered housing schemes.

Under the Care Standards Act 2000, the intention is for care services provided in sheltered and supported housing schemes to be regulated under the domiciliary care agency rather than the care home regulations, thereby recognising the principle that people are still living independent lives in their own homes – as tenants or owners – rather than being in a care home (see section 2.5).

During the passage of the Bill through Parliament there was considerable concern amongst sheltered and supported housing providers that sheltered and supported housing would, perhaps unwittingly, be brought under the care home rather than the domiciliary care regulations in the new Act.

The Act itself does not make the position entirely clear, except to say (s4(3)) that 'domiciliary care agency' means 'arranging the provision of personal care in their own homes for persons who by reason of illness, infirmity or disability are unable to provide it for themselves without assistance'. The key issue is what defines 'own home'.

One way of looking at this, would be to consider the ability of the person to invite or refuse entry to people into their home. If someone is an owner occupier or a tenant they have the legal right to refuse to let someone come into their home. They have control, whereas if someone occupies a room, or suite of rooms, or a property under licence, they do not have a legal right of exclusive possession. In this situation, the person's landlord may gain entry ultimately without that person's consent.

The intentions of the Government are clarified in Hansard in the debate on the Bill. John Hutton, Minister of State at the Department of Health defined the meaning of personal care in the context of a care home:

> 'A care home is defined in clause 3 as an establishment that provides accommodation and nursing [or] personal care for persons who are or who have been ill, who are disabled or infirm or who are or have been dependent on alcohol or drugs.

> '...For an establishment to count as a care home, it must provide assistance with bodily functions, where such assistance is required. It is very important to understand that that does not mean that the personal care provided by the home is limited to assistance with bodily functions; as I have already made clear, the meaning of personal care is to be interpreted more widely than that. The amendment will simply mean that that type of assistance must be available and given if required. Clearly the amount of such assistance that is actually given will depend on the needs of the residents. In a care home for frail elderly people, it is likely to be given fairly often, but in a care home for people with learning disabilities, it might be given only very rarely. However, for an establishment to be registrable as a care home, assistance with bodily functions must be available, even if it is rarely provided. The same requirement is contained in the Registered Homes Act 1984....'

The Minister also makes it clear that:

> 'homes that are currently registered under the 1984 Act should be required to register under the Care Standards Act 2000'.

In the same debate the Minister also clarified, in response to a question, the Government's intention about the regulation of extra care (very sheltered housing) or supported housing:

> 'This is an important issue and the difficulty is that there is no clear definition of sheltered or supported housing. It is technically impossible to state categorically that such accommodation could never be considered to be a care home. However, in almost all such arrangements, care is provided to people in their own homes and that is the essential difference. It is not our intention that someone's own home should be registered as a care home and we are anxious to assure providers that that will remain the position'.

The regulations concerning the implementation of the Act, may clarify this issue.

When must a service be registered as domiciliary care?

The Minister also gave some clarification on the Government's intention in defining domiciliary care in this way, as set out in clause 4(3):

> *'I hope that it is clear from the words "unable to provide it for themselves without assistance" that personal care in this context has a narrower meaning than in the context of a care home. It will clearly include assistance with bodily functions and physical care, which falls short of assistance such as helping a person to get dressed. However, it could not extend to encouragement and emotional support, as that is not a form of personal care that a person could be said to be unable to provide for themselves. Within the normal meaning of the words, a person cannot be said to be either able or unable to provide themselves with emotional support.*

☑ **It is important for providers to be fully aware that the issue of registration for supported and sheltered/very sheltered housing is not yet fully resolved. It would make sense for providers to plan on the basis that in most schemes, any personal care services will come under the domiciliary care regulations. Of critical importance will be whether or not the accommodation provided can be classed as the person's 'own home', since their residents are tenants of their own self-contained flat with their own kitchen and bathroom.**

How will the regulation of domiciliary care agencies relate to housing and floating support services and Supporting People?

For the first time domiciliary care services will operate within a national framework of regulation, through the Care Standards Act 2000. The Act gives a definition of what constitutes a 'domiciliary care service' (see section 2.5). However, the Act does not aim to bring within its remit advice and support functions which do not include a personal care element. This is extremely important for providers, as well as local authorities and the probation service in preparing for the Supporting People arrangements which will be introduced in 2003.

Floating support and other types of information and support services for people in their own homes, that do not include personal care will come under the monitoring arrangements for Supporting People.

Supporting People will establish national standards for support services. It is proposed that providers should self-assess their performance in the context of Best Value and continuous improvement. Local authorities would then commission independent validation checks in consultation with providers. These checks may be annual and would involve visits to services and direct feedback from service users.

☑ **Providers of advice and support services will need to define for themselves whether or not their service includes personal care, as defined in the Act (see section 2.5), in a person's home. This will determine whether or not their service will come under the regulation criteria for domiciliary agencies under the Care Standards Act 2000, or monitoring arrangements for Supporting People.**

How will the Act affect day care providers?

The other main area of the Act which will affect providers of adult services relates to day care. The Act states that regulation may be extended to cover day care services. The Government has stated that it is committed to doing so, though it has given no timescale as yet.

An increasing number of nursing home, residential home and sheltered and supported housing providers also provide some day care services, either for residents they house or for other people in the local area – either on contract or grant aid from local and health authorities, to private self-payers, and sometimes on a voluntary basis through the use of volunteers. In addition, some community-based organisations who do not operate supported housing services, such as domiciliary care providers, and many voluntary organisations such as Age Concern and Mencap, also provide an extensive range of daycare services.

Some of these bodies may not be used to operating within a regulatory environment. In addition, the types of day centre (or day service) in operation vary widely from traditional centres with a focus on care, or occupation, to centres where the focus is more on self-help and enabling.

As in the earlier discussion about defining personal care, some kinds of day services may be offering advice and encouragement rather than personal care services and may not therefore come under the day care regulation when it is introduced.

☑ **Providers of day care services will need to prepare for the possibility of regulation under the Act. In particular, providers should be clear about their aims and objectives, and whether or not the service that they offer has a personal care component.**

4.2 Conclusions, key action and preparation points for service providers

Conclusions

The Act will put in place a new, comprehensive framework of service, training and workforce regulation, designed to improve standards and safeguards for people using care services, and increase public confidence in social care.

New national bodies will be set up – the National Care Standards Commission (April 2002), responsible for the registration and inspection of care services to national standards; and the General Social Care Council (October 2001) to set standards of conduct and practice for staff and employers, and register social workers, managers of residential homes, and other groups of social care staff.

Regulations detailing how the Commission and the Council will work, new codes of practice for staff and employers, and national minimum standards for different types of services, will be issued in draft for consultation before being put into effect.

This guide sets out the main changes to come when the Act is implemented, and more details will be provided in the draft regulations, codes and standards.

Action points now

Independent sector providers, registered social landlords and their managing agents should begin preparing now for the new Act, working together and in conjunction with purchasers, by:

☑ **Considering whether their services provide personal care and, if so, whether care home or domiciliary care agency regulation will apply to them (see 2.5 above).**

☑ **Reviewing the requirements for room sizes and shared rooms in care homes (see 2.8 above) and ways of meeting them by 2007.**

☑ **Checking their personnel procedures and arrangements for recruiting, vetting, appointing and supervising staff, to ensure they can comply with the requirements for protecting vulnerable adults (see 3.7 above).**

☑ **Preparing training strategies for their staff to ensure they will be able to meet required qualification levels by 2005 (see 3.8 above).**

Preparation for the future

As the draft codes and standards emerge, and the Commission and the Council are set up, providers should also:

☑ **Establish contact with the local office of the NCSC and its key personnel, and discuss timescales for implementing changes (see 2.4 above).**

☑ **Assess with inspectors and purchasers, the implications of moving to a single care home, and how best to relate staffing requirements to residents' needs (see 2.5 above).**

☑ **Audit their services against the national standards, identify shortfalls and make plans for implementing required improvements (see 2.8 above).**

☑ **Examine the codes of practice for employers and staff, and ensure they and their staff are able to comply with the requirements (see 3.3 above).**

☑ **Prepare their managers and staff for registration with the GSCC (see 3.4 above).**

Glossary

Care home
Defined in the Care Standards Act 2000 as an establishment providing '...accommodation, together with nursing or personal care, for any of the following persons.
(2) They are – (a) persons who are or have been ill; (b) persons who have or have had a mental disorder; (c) persons who are disabled or infirm; (d) persons who are or have been dependent on alcohol or drugs' (s3(1-2)). Under s121(9), '...an establishment is not a care home...unless the care which it provides includes assistance with bodily functions where such assistance is required'. This definition of a care home includes both residential and nursing homes as defined in the Registered Homes Act 1984.

Caring for People
The Department of Health White Paper (1989) on community care which preceded the NHS and Community Care Act 1990.

Day centre
Defined in the Act (s55(5)) as 'a place where nursing or personal care (but not accommodation) is provided wholly or mainly for persons mentioned in s3(2)' (see under Care home above).

Domiciliary care agency
Under the Act, a local authority or independent sector agency which provides 'personal care in their own homes for persons who by reason of illness, infirmity or disability are unable to provide it for themselves without assistance' (s4(3)).

Fit for the Future
The shorthand title of the Department of Health consultation document *Fit for the Future? National Required Standards for Residential Care and Nursing Homes for Older People* (Department of Health, 1999).

GSCC
Shorthand for the General Social Care Council, which is set up under the Care Standards Act 2000 as the body responsible for setting and regulating standards for staff in England.

Modernising Social Services
The Department of Health White Paper (1998) setting out the Government's policies for social care.

NCSC	Shorthand for the National Care Standards Commission, which is set up under the Act as the statutory national body for regulating services in England.
Personal care	Personal care is not defined in the Care Standards Act 2000, and will have a different meaning in different contexts. In the case of a care home (see above), personal care must include 'assistance with bodily functions where such assistance is required'.
PoCA	Shorthand for the Protection of Children Act 1999, which establishes a statutory list of people considered unsuitable to work with children, in a paid or unpaid capacity. The tribunal set up to hear appeals under this Act will also hear appeals against decisions of the NCSC and the GSCC.
PoVA list	Shorthand for the Protection of Vulnerable Adults list, to be set up under the Care Standards Act (s81) as a statutory list of people considered unsuitable to work with vulnerable adults.
Registered Homes Act 1984 and Registered Homes (Amendment) Act 1991	The current legislation for regulating residential and nursing homes, which the Care Standards Act 2000 replaces.
Sheltered and very sheltered housing	Grouped, self-contained flats or bungalows for older people, usually with communal facilities and warden services. Very sheltered (also known as extra care) housing usually has dedicated care services to support vulnerable older people. Terminology such as category 1, 2 and 2½ is sometimes used to describe different forms of sheltered housing.
Supported housing	Housing for a range of vulnerable groups in either ordinary or specialist housing, where floating or no-site support, and/or care services are provided.
Social care worker	Defined in s55, in relation to the GSCC, as 'a person...who:

(a) engages in relevant social work (...a 'social worker');

(b) is employed at a...care home...or for the purposes of a domiciliary care agency...;

(c) manages an establishment or an agency...mentioned in paragraph (b); or

(d) is supplied by a domiciliary care agency...'; Regulations may add other groups to this list.

Social worker	A person who 'engages in relevant social work' (s55(2)), which is defined as 'social work which is required in connection with any health, education or social services provided by any person' (s55(4)).
Supporting People	The new funding framework which brings together a number of currently separate funding systems for housing related support services for vulnerable people, being introduced by the Government in 2003.
TOPSS England	The national Training Organisation for the Personal Social Services in England, the employment-led body responsible for training strategies and national occupational standards for the social care workforce, including staff and managers in care homes and domiciliary care.